EXPLORE TOGETHER

Resource Book

Lianne Semans Smith & Lee Herdman

Copyright © Scripture Union
First published 2015
ISBN 978 1 78506 027 4

The right of Lianne Semans Smith and Lee Herdman to be identified as authors of this work has been asserted by them in accordance with the Copyright, Designs and Patents Act 1988.

British Library Cataloguing-in-Publication Data: a catalogue record of this book is available from the British Library.

Printed in Malta by Melita Press.

Cover design and internal layout by Jake Howe.

Scripture Union is an international Christian charity working with churches in more than 130 countries.
Thank you for purchasing this resource. Any profits from this book support SU in England and Wales to bring the good news of Jesus Christ to children, young people and families and to enable them to meet God through the Bible and prayer.

Find out more about our work and how you can get involved at:
www.scriptureunion.org.uk (England and Wales)
www.suscotland.org.uk (Scotland)
www.suni.co.uk (Northern Ireland)
www.scriptureunion.org (USA)
www.su.org.au (Australia)

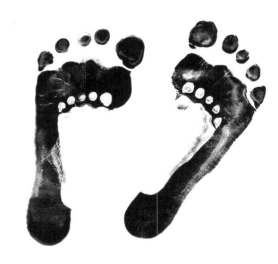

Contents

How to... Explore Together

Within our faith communities there is a rich diversity of God's people all at different stages in their faith development and spiritual experience, and all with different learning needs and preferences. We are a beautiful collection of artists, scholars, reflectors, dancers, data collectors, fact finders, readers, sculptors, writers, musicians, actors, talkers and listeners.

Explore Together places the Bible at the centre of this diversity. It is a new and practical tool for helping people to explore God's Word and hear his voice in a way that embraces their natural preferences. It encourages the community to come together to share their thoughts, questions and revelations with each other. Any and all are welcome and there are no barriers to participation.

At the heart of Explore Together is a desire to see people hear from God and learn more of his love for them. It works with big groups, small groups, mixed-age groups, single-age groups, older people, young people, children, families, house groups, church congregations, youth groups, school groups... in fact, Explore Together can be used in any environment with any group dynamic. It is grounded in years of research and tried and tested in a multitude of contexts.

We're so pleased that you've chosen to buy this resource book. It is designed to equip you and your community as you adventure, journey and grow with God. On this page and the next we have a few suggestions on how to get the most out of the 12 sessions in this resource and how to use the accompanying resources on the Explore Together website (www.exploretogether.org).

Lianne Semans Smith
Lee Herdman

The six steps

There are six essential steps to an Explore Together session, each of which can be tailored to slot into any existing structure and space:

1 **Prepare**
2 **Presenting the Bible**
3 **Pray**
4 **Explore**
5 **Share**
6 **Giving thanks**

These steps are explained in detail in each session outline.

Step 4 provides an opportunity for people to engage with God's Word using the Explore Together questions and the six Explore Together zones. Each zone has been carefully designed to cater for particular learning needs and preferences:

 Colour Zone –
for those who learn by seeing

 Listening Zone –
for those who learn by hearing

 Chat Zone –
for those who learn by thinking aloud

 Word Zone –
for those who learn by reading

 Busy Zone –
for those who learn by doing

 Quiet Zone –
for those who learn by reflecting

Individuals can choose to spend all of their exploring time in one zone, but may also choose to visit several zones, depending upon their preferences. There is no right or wrong amount of time to spend in a zone.

It is quite deliberate that no specific instructions are provided for each zone. Individuals are free to engage however they like with the resources provided in each area as they consider the Explore Together questions for the session.

Basic kit

Although every Explore Together session is different, there are some common elements that are always included. We will refer to these as the 'basic kit' for Explore Together. Before running your first session we advise that you acquire the following items, and top them up as required:

- Explore Together zone signs (available from www.exploretogether.org)
- Explore Together background soundtrack (available from www.exploretogether.org)
- MP3 players (or the means to play downloaded MP3 tracks – eg CDs and CD player)
- plasticine, play dough or clay
- plastic building bricks
- junk modelling items
- pipe cleaners
- pens, pencils and paper
- coloured pencils/pens
- coloured chalk sticks
- pastels/crayons
- glue
- scissors (child-safe)
- masking tape
- white paper
- black paper
- paper of different sorts, sizes and colours
- manuscript paper
- squared paper
- lined paper
- sticky notes
- a selection of Bible commentaries
- a selection of Bibles (different translations)
- children's Bibles and Bible story books, eg *The Big Bible Storybook* (Scripture Union, 2007)
- chairs/cushions/beanbags
- a separate area where people can be quiet

Each session will need a selection of other resources, detailed in Step 1. Many multimedia resources for each session are available for free from www.exploretogether.org/downloads (using the code from the bottom of page 32).

Gathering a team

Although it is entirely possible to lead an Explore Together session alone, it is much more effective when there is a team of people working together to share the responsibility and to model involvement. Strategically placed active participants will encourage others to participate.

The colour, word and busy zones benefit from having a carefully placed team member present to keep the focus on the questions, to engage in the zone activity and to draw people into the questions without dominating. The chat zone requires an experienced host to keep everyone focused.

For detailed team member role descriptions visit www.exploretogether.org.

FAQs

If you have any further questions, it's likely we've answered them in our FAQ section on pages 30 and 31 at the back of this book. If not, please don't hesitate to get in touch via the Scripture Union website: *www.scriptureunion.org.uk.*

If you'd like to know more about the ideas that underpin Explore Together and hear about our experiences of Explore Together in action please read our companion book:

Explore Together: The Journey

Salt and light
Matthew 5:13–16

Themes: teaching, distinctive living, holiness, mission, light

The Sermon on the Mount is thought to have been delivered quite early on in Jesus' ministry. It took place on a mountainside in a town called Capernaum. The crowds gathered to hear what Jesus had to say and they were amazed by his teaching.

Prepare

Resources required
- waves sound effect
- 'Salt and light' sound and fabric introductory story
- 'Salt and light' prayer
- 'Light for the whole world' story text (from *The Big Bible Storybook*)
- 'Light for the whole world' audio recording (from *The Big Bible Storybook* audio book)
- 'Salt and light' image collection
- 'Salt and light' word collection
- Matthew 5:13–16 (CEV)
- 'Salt and light' Explore Together questions (PDF and PowerPoint)

All available from www.exploretogether.org/downloads (using the code from the bottom of page 32).

You will also need to gather:
- a large piece of blue fabric
- audio recordings of different translations of Matthew 5:13–16
- salt in shakers
- coloured craft matchsticks
- items from the Explore Together basic kit (see page 5)
- someone to deliver a short sermon on Matthew 5:13–16 (optional)

Presenting the Bible

With the community gathered together, begin by sharing the words from Matthew 5:13–16. Consider carefully which version of the Bible you choose to read from.

Alternatively or in addition you may choose to use:
- 'Salt and light' sound and fabric introductory story

Without being tempted to answer them, introduce the following questions to your community for them to consider:

- **How do Jesus' words affect you today?**
- **Why does God want you to hear this?**
- **What is God saying to you?**
- **What do you want to say to God?**

Pray

Pray for and with your community, asking God to help you hear from him. This time of prayer can be creative, interactive, responsive, meditative or sung. It could also include communion and intercession. Ensure that there is a place set aside where people can go if they feel that they need someone to pray with them specifically. Have a small team of people available to offer prayer if required. Prayer ministry should be available throughout an Explore Together session.

You may like to use the prayer available on the website.

Explore

Read out your questions from Step 2 again or display them on a screen. Remind your community to consider these questions as they separate into their explore zones. Some may choose to consider all the questions while others may focus on just one. Some may completely ignore the questions and just open themselves up to God.

Invite your community to separate into small groups, around the zone(s) of their preference. Explain that individuals are welcome to spend as much or as little time in each zone as they wish, engaging at whatever level they feel comfortable. Depending upon where your quiet zone is located, you may wish to provide directions and remind people not to disturb one another when using this space.

Colour Zone

- black paper, yellow and white chalk/pastels
- white paper, coloured pastels
- 'Salt and light' image collection
- copies of the 'Salt and light' ET questions

Listening Zone

- 'Light for the whole world' audio recording (from *The Big Bible Storybook* audio book)
- audio recordings of different translations of Matthew 5:13–16
- copies of the 'Salt and light' ET questions
- you may wish to deliver a short sermon in this zone

Chat Zone

- a separate area with chairs, cushions or beanbags
- a chat zone host who is willing to read the passage again and then lead a discussion around the questions
- copies of Matthew 5:13–16 (CEV) or Bibles
- copies of the 'Salt and light' ET questions

Word Zone

- pens, pencils, paper
- biblical commentaries relating to Matthew 5:13–16
- 'Salt and light' word collection
- 'Light for the whole world' story text
- children's Bibles and Bible story books containing a version of Matthew 5:13–16
- copies of Matthew 5:13–16 (CEV) or Bibles
- copies of the 'Salt and light' ET questions

Busy Zone

- plasticine, play dough or clay
- construction blocks of various shapes and sizes
- black paper
- salt in shakers
- coloured craft matchsticks, glue
- copies of the 'Salt and light' ET questions

Quiet Zone

- a separate area where people can be alone with their thoughts and God
- 'Salt and light' image collection (optional)
- copies of Matthew 5:13–16 (CEV) or Bibles
- copies of the 'Salt and light' ET questions

Share

As your time for exploring together draws to a close, invite your community to come back together into small groups of three to five. Suggest that they share their responses to the questions posed at the beginning.

Giving thanks

Invite the explorers to share their reflections with the wider community, drawing together their responses and noting any common themes that emerge. Conclude by reading Matthew 5:13–16 again (from the same Bible version used earlier). Then lead your community in a prayer, thanking God for all that he has revealed through this story. Encourage your community to continue their conversations about this story as they leave, and to take with them any artwork/writings/thoughts from the session.

Worry
Matthew 6:25–34

Themes: provision, prayer, trust, concern, worry, action, harvest

These verses are taken from Jesus' Sermon on the Mount. Jesus was speaking to a large crowd of people about issues that affected their lives. Even though Jesus was speaking thousands of years ago and the same issues still affect our lives today. Worrying can cause so much damage mentally, physically and emotionally. Jesus' teaching helps us to remember that God is the great provider – he knows our needs and will meet them. It is sometimes right to be concerned because healthy concern moves us into action, but worry can be a paralysing force. (This session is suitable for harvest.)

Prepare

Resources required
- 'Mr Worry' short talk
- additional prayer activity
- 'Meditating in the natural world' visual download
- 'You raise me up' audio
- alternative closing activity
- 'Worry' closing PowerPoint
- 'Worry' image collection
- 'Worry' word collection
- Matthew 6:25–34 (CEV)
- 'Worry' Explore Together questions (PDF and PowerPoint)

All available from www.exploretogether.org/downloads (using the code from the bottom of page 32).

You will also need to gather:
- paints and brushes
- ribbons and flags of various colours and lengths
- a vase of highly scented flowers
- *The Very Worried Sparrow* by Meryl Doney (Lion, 2006) or other children's stories on a worry or harvest theme
- 'His eye is on the sparrow' by Free Gospel Band (available from https://itunes.apple.com/gb/album/his-eye-is-on-the-sparrow/id325027684?i=325027911)
- a large backpack
- a number of boxes wrapped in brown paper
- marker pens
- seeds to plant, pots and soil
- pulses, feathers and seeds for collage
- items from the Explore Together basic kit (see page 5)
- someone to deliver a short talk on Matthew 6:25–34 (optional)

Presenting the Bible

With the community gathered together, begin by sharing the words from Matthew 6:25–34. Consider carefully which version of the Bible you choose to read from.

Alternatively or in addition you may choose to use:
- 'Mr Worry' short talk

Without being tempted to answer them, introduce the following questions to your community for them to consider:

- **What are these verses about?**
- **What do they tell us about trusting God?**
- **How do you feel about God as your provider?**
- **What does God want you to do?**

Pray

Pray for and with your community, asking God to help you hear from him. This time of prayer can be creative, interactive, responsive, meditative or sung. It could also include communion and intercession. Ensure that there is a place set aside where people can go if they feel that they need someone to pray with them specifically. Have a small team of people available to offer prayer if required. Prayer ministry should be available throughout an Explore Together session.

Explore

Read out your questions from Step 2 again or display them on a screen. Remind your community to consider these questions as they separate into their explore zones. Some may choose to consider all the questions while others may focus on just one. Some may completely ignore the questions and just open themselves up to God.

Invite your community to separate into small groups, around the zone(s) of their preference. Explain that individuals are welcome to spend as much or as little time in each zone as they wish, engaging at whatever level they feel comfortable. Depending upon where your quiet zone is located, you may wish to provide directions and remind people not to disturb one another when using this space.

Colour Zone
- paint, brushes and paper
- coloured pastels, crayons and white paper
- flags and ribbons of different colours and lengths, for dancing/moving with
- a vase of highly scented flowers
- 'Worry' image collection
- copies of the 'Worry' ET questions

Listening Zone
- MP3 players with 'You raise me up' audio
- MP3 players with 'His eye is on the sparrow'
- *The Very Worried Sparrow* by Meryl Doney, or other children's stories on a harvest theme, to read aloud
- copies of the 'Worry' ET questions
- a talk or sermon based on this passage could be shared

Chat Zone
- a separate area with chairs, cushions or beanbags
- a chat zone host who is willing to read the passage again and then lead a discussion around the questions
- copies of Matthew 6:25–34 (CEV) or Bibles
- copies of the 'Worry' ET questions

Word Zone
- pens and pencils
- plain paper of different sizes, ruled and squared paper
- biblical commentaries relating to Matthew 6:25–34
- *The Very Worried Sparrow* by Meryl Doney, or other children's stories on a harvest theme
- 'Worry' word collection
- copies of Matthew 6:25–34 (CEV) or Bibles
- copies of the 'Worry' ET questions

Busy Zone

- plasticine, play dough or clay
- seeds to plant, pots and soil
- scissors, glue, feathers, pulses and seeds for collage
- paper
- copies of the 'Worry' ET questions

Quiet Zone

- a separate area where people can be alone with their thoughts and God
- 'Worry' image collection (optional)
- copies of Matthew 6:25–34 (CEV) or Bibles
- copies of the 'Worry' ET questions

Share

As your time for exploring together draws to a close, invite your community to come back together into small groups of three to five. Suggest that they share their responses to the questions posed at the beginning.

Giving thanks

Invite the explorers to share their reflections with the wider community, drawing together their responses and noting any common themes that emerge. Conclude by reading Matthew 6:25–34 again (from the same Bible version used earlier). Then lead your community in a prayer, thanking God for all that he has revealed through this story. Alternatively, use the closing activity from the website. Encourage your community to continue their conversations about this story as they leave, and to take with them any artwork/writings/thoughts from the session.

Jesus calms the storm

Mark 4:35–41

Themes: faith, trust, storms, tension, worry, fear, miracles, calm

In this passage, Jesus, seeking to escape the noisy crowds, invites his disciples to take a short boat trip with him across the lake. The ensuing storm reveals the disciples' lack of faith and trust in Jesus while setting the scene for yet another incredible miracle.

Prepare

Resources required
- Visio Divina prompt sheet
- 'On the Sea of Galilee' poem text
- 'Jesus calms the storm' parachute story
- 'Jesus stops a storm' audio recording (from *The Big Bible* Storybook audio book)
- 'On the Sea of Galilee' poem, audio recording
- stormy seas image collection
- calm seas image collection
- stormy seas word collection
- Mark 4:35–41 (CEV)
- 'Jesus calms the storm' Explore Together questions (PDF and PowerPoint)

All available from www.exploretogether.org/downloads (using the code from the bottom of page 32).

You will also need to gather:
- blue fabric, blue ribbons, of different shades and lengths, for dancing and moving with
- audio versions of different translations of Mark 4:35–41
- items from the Explore Together basic kit (see page 5)

Presenting the Bible

With the community gathered together, begin by sharing the words from Mark 4:35–41. Consider carefully which version of the Bible you choose to read from.

Alternatively or in addition you may choose to use one of the following:
- 'On the Sea of Galilee' poem
- Visio Divina
- 'Jesus calms the storm' parachute story

Without being tempted to answer them, introduce the following questions to your community for them to consider:

- **What does this story tell us about Jesus?**
- **What is Jesus saying to you through this story?**
- **What storms are raging around you?**
- **When have you had to trust that Jesus is in control?**

Pray

Pray for and with your community, asking God to help you hear from him. This time of prayer can be creative, interactive, responsive, meditative or sung. It could also include communion and intercession. Ensure that there is a place set aside where people can go if they feel that they need someone to pray with them specifically. Have a small team of people available to offer prayer if required. Prayer ministry should be available throughout an Explore Together session.

Explore

Read out your questions from Step 2 again or display them on a screen. Remind your community to consider these questions as they separate into their explore zones. Some may choose to consider all the questions while others may focus on just one. Some may completely ignore the questions and just open themselves up to God.

Invite your community to separate into small groups, around the zone(s) of their preference. Explain that individuals are welcome to spend as much or as little time in each zone as they wish, engaging at whatever level they feel comfortable. Depending upon where your quiet zone is located, you may wish to provide directions and remind people not to disturb one another when using this space.

Colour Zone
- coloured chalk sticks, glue and black paper
- coloured pastels, crayons and white paper
- stormy seas image collection
- calm seas image collection
- Visio Divina prompt sheet
- blue fabric, blue ribbons, of different shades and lengths, for dancing and moving with
- copies of the 'Jesus calms the storm' ET questions

Listening Zone
- MP3 players with recording of the poem 'On the Sea of Galilee'
- 'Jesus stops a storm' audio recording (from *The Big Bible Storybook* audio book)
- audio versions of different translations of Mark 4:35–41
- copies of the 'Jesus calms the storm' ET questions

Chat Zone
- a separate area with chairs, cushions or beanbags
- a chat zone host who is willing to read the passage again and then lead a discussion around the questions
- copies of Mark 4:35–41 (CEV) or Bibles
- copies of the 'Jesus calms the storm' ET questions

Word Zone
- pens, pencils, paper, commentaries
- 'On the Sea of Galilee' poem text
- stormy seas word collection
- copies of *The Big Bible Storybook* open at 'Jesus stops a storm', or other children's Bibles and Bible story books containing a version of Mark 4:35–41
- copies of the 'Jesus calms the storm' ET questions

Busy Zone
- plasticine, play dough or clay
- plastic building bricks
- junk modelling items
- masking tape, glue and scissors
- copies of the 'Jesus calms the storm' ET questions

Quiet Zone
- a separate area where people can be alone with their thoughts and God
- stormy seas image collection (optional)
- calm seas image collection (optional)
- copies of Mark 4:35–41 (CEV) or Bibles
- copies of the 'Jesus calms the storm' ET questions

Share

As your time for exploring together draws to a close, invite your community to come back together into small groups of three to five. Suggest that they share their responses to the questions posed at the beginning.

Giving thanks

Invite the explorers to share their reflections with the wider community, drawing together their responses and noting any common themes that emerge. Conclude by reading Mark 4:35–41 again (from the same Bible version used earlier). Then lead your community in a prayer, thanking God for all that he has revealed through this story. Encourage your community to continue their conversations about this story as they leave, and to take with them any artwork/writings/thoughts from the session.

The birth of Jesus
Luke 1:26–38; 2:1–21

Themes: Christmas, nativity, birth, Jesus, incarnation, God with us, God's love

The story of the first Christmas and the birth of Jesus within the Gospels is only a small part of the earthly life of Jesus, which is in turn a small part of a much bigger story. The big story tells us that Jesus has existed for all eternity, that he came to be 'flesh and bones', 'totally human – totally God' who walks with us, is close to us and rescues us. Then, more than this, he continues to be with us through the presence of the Holy Spirit, drawing us into an eternity with him. Within this Explore Together session, it is important that those gathering can see the bigger context of this well known passage – it is much more than a story about a baby in a stable and a bunch of shepherds visiting, it is the story of a God who passionately loves and wants to be with his people.

Prepare

Resources required
- The birth of Jesus' rhyme (PDF and PowerPoint)
- 'The birth of Jesus' story with key words and actions
- nativity characters
- 'A message for Mary' audio recording (from *The Big Bible* Storybook audio book)
- 'A message for the shepherds' audio recording (from *The Big Bible Storyboo*k audio book)
- 'The birth of Jesus' image collection
- Christmas carols word collection
- Luke 1:26–38; 2:1–21 (CEV)
- 'The birth of Jesus' Explore Together questions (PDF and PowerPoint)

All available from www.exploretogether.org/downloads (using the code from the bottom of page 32).

You will also need to gather:
- ribbons and flags of various colours and lengths
- one or two 'story sharers' – individuals chosen to share their own testimony about God being with them. These individuals might be sat around the chat zone or listening zone, ready to tell their story and answer questions, or be spread around the room. The story sharers should have something to help people recognise their role, eg hold a character from a nativity set or wear a piece of tinsel
- items from the Explore Together basic kit (see page 5)

Presenting the Bible

With the community gathered together, begin by sharing the words from Luke 1:26–38 and 2:1–21. Consider carefully which version of the Bible you choose to read from.

Alternatively or in addition you may choose to use one of the following:
- 'The birth of Jesus' rhyme (PDF and PowerPoint)
- 'The birth of Jesus' story with key words and actions

Without being tempted to answer them, introduce the following questions to your community for them to consider:

- **Why would God choose to be a baby?**
- **When has God been with you?**
- **What difference does it make to people that God is with them?**
- **How will you help others know that God is with them?**

Pray

Pray for and with your community, asking God to help you hear from him. This time of prayer can be creative, interactive, responsive, meditative or sung. It could also include communion and intercession. Ensure that there is a place set aside where people can go if they feel that they need someone to pray with them specifically. Have a small team of people available to offer prayer if required. Prayer ministry should be available throughout an Explore Together session.

Explore

Read out your questions from Step 2 again or display them on a screen. Remind your community to consider these questions as they separate into their explore zones. Some may choose to consider all the questions while others may focus on just one. Some may completely ignore the questions and just open themselves up to God.

Invite your community to separate into small groups, around the zone(s) of their preference. Explain that individuals are welcome to spend as much or as little time in each zone as they wish, engaging at whatever level they feel comfortable. Depending upon where your quiet zone is located, you may wish to provide directions and remind people not to disturb one another when using this space.

Colour Zone
- coloured chalk sticks, glue and black paper
- coloured pastels, crayons and white paper
- flags and ribbons of different colours and lengths, for dancing/moving with
- 'The birth of Jesus' image collection
- copies of the 'The birth of Jesus' ET questions

Listening Zone
- 'A message for Mary' audio recording (from *The Big Bible Storybook* audio book)
- 'A message for the shepherds' audio recording (from *The Big Bible Storybook* audio book)
- one or two story sharers (see Step 1 resource list)
- copies of the 'The birth of Jesus' ET questions

Chat Zone
- a separate area with chairs, cushions or beanbags
- a chat zone host who is willing to read the passage again and then lead a discussion around the questions
- one or two story sharers (see Step 1 resource list)
- copies of Luke 1:26–38; 2:1–21 (CEV) or Bibles
- copies of the 'The birth of Jesus' ET questions

Word Zone
- pens and pencils
- plain paper of different sizes, ruled and squared paper
- biblical commentaries relating to Luke 1:26–38 and 2:1–21
- Christmas carol word collection
- copies of *The Big Bible Storybook* open at 'A message for Mary'/'A message for the shepherds', or other children's Bibles and Bible story books containing a version of Luke 1:26–38; 2:1–21
- copies of Luke 1:26–38; 2:1–21 (CEV) or Bibles
- 'The birth of Jesus' rhyme
- copies of the 'The birth of Jesus' ET questions

Busy Zone
- plasticine, play dough or clay
- construction blocks
- junk modelling items
- copies of the 'The birth of Jesus' ET questions

Quiet Zone
- a separate area where people can be alone with their thoughts and God
- 'The birth of Jesus' image collection (optional)
- copies of Luke 1:26–38; 2:1–21 (CEV) or Bibles
- copies of the 'The birth of Jesus' ET questions

Share

As your time for exploring together draws to a close, invite your community to come back together into small groups of three to five. Suggest that they share their responses to the questions posed at the beginning.

Giving thanks

Invite the explorers to share their reflections with the wider community, drawing together their responses and noting any common themes that emerge. Conclude by reading Luke 1:26–38 and 2:1–21 again (from the same Bible version used earlier). Then lead your community in a prayer, thanking God for all that he has revealed through this story. Encourage your community to continue their conversations about this story as they leave, and to take with them any artwork/writings/thoughts from the session.

Simeon and Anna

Luke 2:21–38 Themes: celebration, Christmas, thanksgiving, prophesy, salvation, blessing

Forty days after Jesus had been born his parents took him to the Temple to present him to God, as was the Jewish custom. Upon arriving at the Temple, Joseph and Mary encountered Simeon and Anna who gave thanks for Jesus and spoke of his future.

Prepare

Resources required
- Simeon and Anna's monologues
- 'Simeon and Anna' audio recording (from *The Big Bible Storybook* audio book)
- 'Simeon and Anna' story text (from *The Big Bible Storybook*)
- additional prayer activity
- incarnation quotes word collection
- 'Simeon and Anna' image collection
- light image collection
- Luke 2:21–38 (CEV)
- 'Simeon and Anna' Explore Together questions (PDF and PowerPoint)

All available from www.exploretogether.org/downloads (using the code from the bottom of page 32).

You will also need to gather:
- a recording of the Nunc Dimittis (Simeon's song) – various versions of this song are available; choose one that best suits (or perhaps challenges!) your community
- Scratch Art doodle sheets
- a selection of used Christmas cards (both nativity and non-nativity)
- glitter
- beads and thread
- embroidery silks, aida fabric, threads and blunt needles
- items from the Explore Together basic kit (see page 5)

Presenting the Bible

With the community gathered together, begin by sharing the words from Luke 2:21–38. Consider carefully which version of the Bible you choose to read from.

Alternatively or in addition you may choose to use:
- Simeon and Anna's monologues

Without being tempted to answer them, introduce the following questions to your community for them to consider:

- **Why is this story good news for you?**
- **Why is this story good news for your neighbours?**
- **How can you be a light that draws all mankind to God?**
- **How can we as a community be a light that draws all mankind to God?**

Pray

Pray for and with your community, asking God to help you hear from him. This time of prayer can be creative, interactive, responsive, meditative or sung. It could also include communion and intercession. Ensure that there is a place set aside where people can go if they feel that they need someone to pray with them specifically. Have a small team of people available to offer prayer if required. Prayer ministry should be available throughout an Explore Together session.

Explore

Read out your questions from Step 2 again or display them on a screen. Remind your community to consider these questions as they separate into their explore zones. Some may choose to consider all the questions while others may focus on just one. Some may completely ignore the questions and just open themselves up to God.

Invite your community to separate into small groups, around the zone(s) of their preference. Explain that individuals are welcome to spend as much or as little time in each zone as they wish, engaging at whatever level they feel comfortable. Depending upon where your quiet zone is located, you may wish to provide directions and remind people not to disturb one another when using this space.

Colour Zone
- coloured pastels, crayons and various colours and sizes of paper
- 'Simeon and Anna' image collection
- light image collection
- Scratch Art doodle sheets
- used Christmas cards, glue, scissors and glitter for collage
- copies of the 'Simeon and Anna' ET questions

Listening Zone
- 'Simeon and Anna' audio recording (from *The Big Bible Storybook* audio book)
- a recording of the Nunc Dimittis
- copies of the 'Simeon and Anna' ET questions

Chat Zone
- a separate area with chairs, cushions or beanbags
- a chat zone host who is willing to read the passage again and then lead a discussion around the questions
- copies of Luke 2:21–38 (CEV) or Bibles
- copies of the 'Simeon and Anna' ET questions

Word Zone

- pens, pencils, paper
- biblical commentaries relating to Luke 2:21–38
- 'Simeon and Anna' story text
- other children's Bibles and Bible story books containing a version of Luke 2:21–38
- 'Simeon and Anna' story text (from *The Big Bible Storybook*)
- copies of Luke 2:21–38 (CEV) or Bibles
- incarnation quotes word collection
- copies of the 'Simeon and Anna' ET questions

Busy Zone
- plasticine, play dough or clay
- pipe cleaners
- beads and thread
- embroidery silks, aida fabric, threads and blunt needles
- junk modelling items
- masking tape, glue and scissors
- copies of the 'Simeon and Anna' ET questions

Quiet Zone
- a separate area where people can be alone with their thoughts and God
- 'Simeon and Anna' image collection (optional)
- light image collection (optional)
- copies of Luke 2:21–38 (CEV) or Bibles
- copies of the 'Simeon and Anna' ET questions

Share

As your time for exploring together draws to a close, invite your community to come back together into small groups of three to five. Suggest that they share their responses to the questions posed at the beginning.

Giving thanks

Invite the explorers to share their reflections with the wider community, drawing together their responses and noting any common themes that emerge. Conclude by reading Luke 2:21–38 again (from the same Bible version used earlier). Then lead your community in a prayer, thanking God for all that he has revealed through this story. Encourage your community to continue their conversations about this story as they leave, and to take with them any artwork/writings/thoughts from the session.

The great feast
Luke 14:15–24

Themes: parable, kingdom, heaven, inclusivity, the poor, a feast

Jesus teaches about the kingdom of heaven by telling a story about a feast. Those who are invited make excuses not to come, so the master goes on to invite everyone who can be found in the streets and the alleyways – no one is left out.

Prepare

Resources required
- 'The great feast' story with visuals (PDF and PowerPoint)
- 'The great feast' story and song
- 'Come to the party' audio recording (from *The Big Bible Storybook* audio book)
- 'The great feast' suggested teaching outline (PDF and PowerPoint)
- 'I'm invited?' poem
- 'I'm invited?' poem audio
- Bible verses
- 'The great feast' image collection
- 'The great feast' word collection
- Luke 14:15–24 (CEV)
- 'The great feast' Explore Together questions (PDF and PowerPoint)

All available from www.exploretogether.org/downloads (using the code from the bottom of page 32).

You will also need to gather:
- ribbons and flags of various colours and lengths
- gold and metallic paper, silver tin foil, craft jewels
- audio versions of different translations of Luke 14:15–24
- items from the Explore Together basic kit (see page 5)
- someone to deliver a short message on Luke 14:15–24 (optional)

Presenting the Bible

With the community gathered together, begin by sharing the words from Luke 14:15–24. Consider carefully which version of the Bible you choose to read from.

Alternatively or in addition you may choose to use one of the following:
- 'The great feast' story with visuals (PDF and PowerPoint)
- 'The great feast' story and song
- 'Come to the party' audio recording (from *The Big Bible Storybook* audio book)

Without being tempted to answer them, introduce the following questions to your community for them to consider:

- **What is Jesus saying to you when he tells this story?**
- **Who needs to be invited? How will you invite them?**
- **Do you recognise yourself, or anyone you know, as a character in the story?**
- **When you meet Jesus at the great feast, what words will you speak?**

Pray

Pray for and with your community, asking God to help you hear from him. This time of prayer can be creative, interactive, responsive, meditative or sung. It could also include communion and intercession. Ensure that there is a place set aside where people can go if they feel that they need someone to pray with them specifically. Have a small team of people available to offer prayer if required. Prayer ministry should be available throughout an Explore Together session.

Explore

Read out your questions from Step 2 again or display them on a screen. Remind your community to consider these questions as they separate into their explore zones. Some may choose to consider all the questions while others may focus on just one. Some may completely ignore the questions and just open themselves up to God.

Invite your community to separate into small groups, around the zone(s) of their preference. Explain that individuals are welcome to spend as much or as little time in each zone as they wish, engaging at whatever level they feel comfortable. Depending upon where your quiet zone is located, you may wish to provide directions and remind people not to disturb one another when using this space.

Colour Zone
- coloured chalk sticks, glue and black paper
- coloured pastels, crayons and white paper
- scissors
- gold and metallic paper, silver tin foil, craft jewels
- flags and ribbons of different colours and lengths, for dancing/moving with
- 'The great feast' image collection
- copies of the 'The great feast' ET questions

Listening Zone
- 'Come to the party' audio recording (from *The Big Bible Storybook* audio book)
- audio versions of different translations of Luke 14:15–24
- 'I'm invited?' poem audio
- copies of the 'The great feast' ET questions
- you may wish to deliver a short message on Luke 14:15–24

Chat Zone
- a separate area with chairs, cushions or beanbags
- a chat zone host who is willing to read the passage again and then lead a discussion around the questions
- copies of Luke 14:15–24 (CEV) or Bibles
- copies of the 'The great feast' ET questions

Word Zone
- pens, pencils
- plain paper of different sizes, ruled and squared paper
- biblical commentaries relating to Luke 14:15–24
- 'The great feast' word collection
- copies of *The Big Bible Storybook* open at 'Come to the party', or other children's Bibles and Bible story books containing a version of Luke 14:15–24
- copies of Luke 14:15–24 (CEV) or Bibles
- Bible verses
- copies of 'I'm invited?' poem
- copies of the 'The great feast' ET questions

Busy Zone
- plasticine, play dough or clay
- plastic building bricks
- junk modelling items
- copies of the 'The great feast' ET questions

Quiet Zone
- a separate area where people can be alone with their thoughts and God
- 'The great feast' image collection (optional)
- copies of Luke 14:15–24 (CEV) or Bibles
- copies of the 'The great feast' ET questions

Share

As your time for exploring together draws to a close, invite your community to come back together into small groups of three to five. Suggest that they share their responses to the questions posed at the beginning.

Giving thanks

Invite the explorers to share their reflections with the wider community, drawing together their responses and noting any common themes that emerge. Conclude by reading Luke 14:15–24 again (from the same Bible version used earlier). Then lead your community in a prayer, thanking God for all that he has revealed through this story. Encourage your community to continue their conversations about this story as they leave, and to take with them any artwork/writings/thoughts from the session.

Easter
Luke 24:1–12

Themes: Easter, resurrection, promises, awe and wonder, God's power, salvation, victory

Early one morning, three days after Jesus had died on the cross, some women went to visit his tomb to take care of his body. When they arrived they were terrified to see that Jesus' body was missing, leaving only scraps of linen behind. To their amazement, they discovered that Jesus had risen from the dead, just as he had said. You might wish to begin your time of worship with the exchange available on the website.

Prepare

Resources required
- worship exchange (PDF and PowerPoint)
- 'Resurrection' interview
- 'Easter' cartoon
- 'Easter story' animation
- 'Easter quotes' PowerPoint
- 'Jesus is alive!' audio recording (from *The Big Bible Storybook* audio book)
- 'Easter' prayer idea
- 'Easter' extra idea
- 'Easter' image collection
- 'Easter' word collection
- Luke 24:1–12 (CEV)
- 'Easter' Explore Together questions (PDF and PowerPoint)

All available from www.exploretogether.org/downloads (using the code from the bottom of page 32).

You will also need to gather:
- a vase of fresh, colourful, sweet-smelling flowers
- lining paper in the shape of a cross
- plain white paper crosses
- trays of natural resources for gardens, collages, sculptures and play (eg grass, flowers, leaves, rocks, twigs, clay, soil)
- coloured beads and thread
- audio versions of different translations of Luke 24:1–12
- items from the Explore Together basic kit (see page 5)
- someone to deliver a short sermon on Luke 24:1–12 (optional)

Presenting the Bible

With the community gathered together, begin by sharing the words from Luke 24:1–12. Consider carefully which version of the Bible you choose to read from.

Alternatively or in addition you may choose to use one of the following:
- 'Easter quotes' PowerPoint
- 'Easter story' animation
- 'Resurrection' interview

Without being tempted to answer them, introduce the following questions to your community for them to consider:

- **How do you know that Jesus is alive?**
- **What difference does knowing this story make to your life? (Your family, friends, school, workplace?)**
- **Now that you have heard the Easter story again, what do you want to say to God?**
- **What have you learned about this story that you didn't know before?**

Pray

Pray for and with your community, asking God to help you hear from him. This time of prayer can be creative, interactive, responsive, meditative or sung. It could also include communion and intercession. Ensure that there is a place set aside where people can go if they feel that they need someone to pray with them specifically. Have a small team of people available to offer prayer if required. Prayer ministry should be available throughout an Explore Together session.

Explore

Read out your questions from Step 2 again or display them on a screen. Remind your community to consider these questions as they separate into their explore zones. Some may choose to consider all the questions while others may focus on just one. Some may completely ignore the questions and just open themselves up to God.

Invite your community to separate into small groups, around the zone(s) of their preference. Explain that individuals are welcome to spend as much or as little time in each zone as they wish, engaging at whatever level they feel comfortable. Depending upon where your quiet zone is located, you may wish to provide directions and remind people not to disturb one another when using this space.

Colour Zone

- white paper, coloured pencils and pens
- lining paper in the shape of a cross
- a vase of fresh, colourful, sweet-smelling flowers
- copies of the 'Easter' cartoon
- 'Easter' image collection
- copies of the 'Easter' ET questions

Listening Zone

- 'Jesus is alive!' audio recording (from *The Big Bible Storybook* audio book)
- audio versions of different translations of Luke 24:1–12
- copies of the 'Easter' ET questions
- you may wish to deliver a short sermon in this zone

Chat Zone
- a separate area with chairs, cushions or beanbags
- a chat zone host who is willing to read the passage again and then lead a discussion around the questions
- copies of Luke 24:1–12 (CEV) or Bibles
- copies of the 'Easter' ET questions

Word Zone

- pens, pencils, paper
- biblical commentaries relating to Luke 24:1–12
- 'Easter' word collection
- copies of *The Big Bible Storybook* open at 'Jesus is alive!', or other children's Bibles and Bible story books containing a version of Luke 24:1–12
- copies of Luke 24:1–12 (CEV) or Bibles
- plain white paper crosses
- copies of the 'Easter' ET questions

Busy Zone

- trays of natural resources for gardens, collages, sculptures and play (eg grass, flowers, leaves, rocks, twigs, clay, soil)
- coloured beads and thread
- copies of the 'Easter' cartoon (cut up and muddle the frames and challenge individuals to re-order them)
- copies of the 'Easter' ET questions

Quiet Zone
- a separate area where people can be alone with their thoughts and God
- 'Easter' image collection (optional)
- copies of Luke 24:1–12 (CEV, printed sheet) or Bibles
- copies of the 'Easter' ET questions

Share

As your time for exploring together draws to a close, invite your community to come back together into small groups of three to five. Suggest that they share their responses to the questions posed at the beginning.

Giving thanks

Invite the explorers to share their reflections with the wider community, drawing together their responses and noting any common themes that emerge. Conclude by reading Luke 24:1–12 again (from the same Bible version used earlier). Then lead your community in a prayer, thanking God for all that he has revealed through this story. Encourage your community to continue their conversations about this story as they leave, and to take with them any artwork/writings/thoughts from the session.

Jesus and Nicodemus

John 3:1–21   Themes: questions, doubts, need, faith, the Holy Spirit

Nicodemus sneaked out to find Jesus at night, with some of the questions that he needed to have answered. He did not go away disappointed. Jesus had the answers to Nicodemus' biggest questions.

Prepare

Resources required
- 'The story of Nicodemus' active listening story sheet
- 'Jesus and Nicodemus' picture activity
- 'Jesus and Nicodemus' puppets
- 'Jesus and Nicodemus' suggested teaching outline
- 'An evening visitor' audio recording (from *The Big Bible Storybook* audio book)
- 'An evening visitor' story text (from *The Big Bible Storybook*)
- 'Quiet visits' audio
- 'Jesus and Nicodemus' image collection
- 'Jesus and Nicodemus' word collection
- John 3:1–21 (CEV)
- 'Jesus and Nicodemus' Explore Together questions (PDF and PowerPoint)

All available from www.exploretogether.org/downloads (using the code from the bottom of page 32).

You will also need to gather:

- coloured flags and/or ribbons for dancing/moving with
- white chalk
- rough hewn wood and squares of sandpaper
- small scrolls of paper
- items from the Explore Together basic kit (see page 5)
- someone to deliver a short talk about John 3:1–21, using the suggested teaching outline, if desired (optional)

Presenting the Bible

With the community gathered together, begin by sharing the words from John 3:1–21. Consider carefully which version of the Bible you choose to read from. You may wish to use the music from the audio recording 'Quiet visits'.

Alternatively or in addition you may choose to use one of the following:
- 'The story of Nicodemus' active listening story sheet
- retell the story of Jesus and Nicodemus using the 'Jesus and Nicodemus' picture activity or puppets

Without being tempted to answer them, introduce the following questions to your community for them to consider:

- **What question would you like to ask Jesus?**
- **What is Jesus saying to you?**
- **When have you needed Jesus and known he is there?**
- **What questions are others around you asking? How can you help answer their questions?**

Pray

Pray for and with your community, asking God to help you hear from him. This time of prayer can be creative, interactive, responsive, meditative or sung. It could also include communion and intercession. Ensure that there is a place set aside where people can go if they feel that they need someone to pray with them specifically. Have a small team of people available to offer prayer if required. Prayer ministry should be available throughout an Explore Together session.

Explore

Read out your questions from Step 2 again or display them on a screen. Remind your community to consider these questions as they separate into their explore zones. Some may choose to consider all the questions while others may focus on just one. Some may completely ignore the questions and just open themselves up to God.

Invite your community to separate into small groups, around the zone(s) of their preference. Explain that individuals are welcome to spend as much or as little time in each zone as they wish, engaging at whatever level they feel comfortable. Depending upon where your quiet zone is located, you may wish to provide directions and remind people not to disturb one another when using this space.

Colour Zone
- coloured chalk sticks, glue and black paper
- white chalk and black paper (to explore living in the light and dark, and coming to Jesus at night)
- coloured pastels, crayons and white paper
- 'Jesus and Nicodemus' image collection
- copies of the 'Jesus and Nicodemus' ET questions

Listening Zone
- MP3 players with the 'Quiet visits' audio recording
- 'An evening visitor' audio recording (from *The Big Bible Storybook* audio book)
- copies of the 'Jesus and Nicodemus' ET questions
- you may wish to deliver a short talk in this zone

Chat Zone

- a separate area with chairs, cushions or beanbags
- a chat zone host who is willing to read the passage again and then lead a discussion around the questions
- copies of John 3:1–21 (CEV) or Bibles
- copies of the 'Jesus and Nicodemus' ET questions

Word Zone
- pens, pencils, paper
- biblical commentaries relating to John 3:1–21
- 'Jesus and Nicodemus' word collection
- 'An evening visitor' story text
- other children's Bibles and Bible story books containing a version of John 3:1–21
- copies of John 3:1–21 (CEV) or Bibles
- 'Jesus and Nicodemus' suggested teaching outline
- small scrolls of paper for writing questions on
- copies of the 'Jesus and Nicodemus' ET questions

Busy Zone
- plasticine, play dough or clay
- plastic bricks
- junk modelling items
- rough hewn wood and small squares of sandpaper
- ribbons and flags of various colours for dancing/moving with
- copies of the 'Jesus and Nicodemus' ET questions

Quiet Zone

- a separate area where people can be alone with their thoughts and God
- 'Jesus and Nicodemus' image collection (optional)
- copies of John 3:1–21 (CEV, printed sheet) or Bibles
- copies of the 'Jesus and Nicodemus' ET questions

Share

As your time for exploring together draws to a close, invite your community to come back together into small groups of three to five. Suggest that they share their responses to the questions posed at the beginning.

Giving thanks

Invite the explorers to share their reflections with the wider community, drawing together their responses and noting any common themes that emerge. Conclude by reading John 3:1–21 again (from the same Bible version used earlier). Then lead your community in a prayer, thanking God for all that he has revealed through this story. Encourage your community to continue their conversations about this story as they leave, and to take with them any artwork/writings/thoughts from the session.

Pentecost!

Acts 2   Themes: Pentecost, celebration, the church, the Holy Spirit, receiving from God

In this passage God keeps his promise. His people are not on their own; he is with them. His people are not powerless; the Holy Spirit gives them his power. Before Pentecost only a small number of followers had God the Holy Spirit with them; on the day of Pentecost, everyone (men, women, boys, girls, young, old) was filled with the Holy Spirit. He was there to help them live with his power.

Prepare

Resources required
- Pentecost animations 1 and 2
- 'Interviewing Peter' script
- 'Pentecost!' suggested teaching outline
- 'Early one morning' audio recording (from *The Big Bible Storybook* audio book)
- 'Early one morning' story text (from *The Big Bible Storybook*)
- 'A Pentecost rhyme'
- 'Pentecost!' image collection
- 'Pentecost!' word collection
- Acts 2 (CEV)
- 'Pentecost!' Explore Together questions

All available from www.exploretogether.org/downloads (using the code from the bottom of page 32).

You will also need to gather:
- coloured flags and ribbons for moving with (maybe making red, orange and yellow ribbons and flags)
- paints
- thick red/orange/yellow felt tips
- red, orange and yellow paper/scraps
- rough hewn wood and small squares of sandpaper
- items from the Explore Together basic kit (see page 5)
- someone to deliver a short sermon on Acts 2, using the suggested teaching outline, if desired (optional)

Presenting the Bible

With the community gathered together, begin by sharing the words from Acts 2. Consider carefully which version of the Bible you choose to read from.

Alternatively or in addition you may choose to use one of the following:
- 'Interviewing Peter' script
- Pentecost animation 1 (Have someone read the words for those who struggle to read. You might wish to invite individuals who speak different languages to say 'God is love' in their own language.)
- Pentecost animation 2

Without being tempted to answer them, introduce the following questions to your community for them to consider:

- **Why do you need God the Holy Spirit?**
- **How will you know when you are full of the Holy Spirit?**
- **What is God the Holy Spirit saying to you?**
- **How is God the Holy Spirit at work in your life?**

Pray

Pray for and with your community, asking God to help you hear from him. This time of prayer can be creative, interactive, responsive, meditative or sung. It could also include communion and intercession. Ensure that there is a place set aside where people can go if they feel that they need someone to pray with them specifically. Have a small team of people available to offer prayer if required. Prayer ministry should be available throughout an Explore Together session.

Explore

Read out your questions from Step 2 again or display them on a screen. Remind your community to consider these questions as they separate into their explore zones. Some may choose to consider all the questions while others may focus on just one. Some may completely ignore the questions and just open themselves up to God.

Invite your community to separate into small groups, around the zone(s) of their preference. Explain that individuals are welcome to spend as much or as little time in each zone as they wish, engaging at whatever level they feel comfortable. Depending upon where your quiet zone is located, you may wish to provide directions and remind people not to disturb one another when using this space.

Colour Zone
- coloured chalk sticks, glue and black paper
- coloured pastels, crayons and white paper
- paints, crayons, pastels, thick felt tips that are red, yellow and orange
- red, yellow and orange paper/scraps, scissors and glue, for use in collage
- 'Pentecost!' image collection
- copies of the 'Pentecost!' ET questions

Listening Zone
- 'Early one morning' audio recording (from *The Big Bible Storybook* audio book)
- copies of the 'Pentecost!' ET questions
- you may wish to deliver a short sermon in this zone

Chat Zone
- a separate area with chairs, cushions or beanbags
- a chat zone host who is willing to read the passage again and then lead a discussion around the questions
- copies of Acts 2 (CEV) or Bibles
- copies of the 'Pentecost!' ET questions

Word Zone
- pens, pencils, paper
- an individual to teach 'A Pentecost rhyme' to those who would like to hear it and learn it

- 'Pentecost!' suggested teaching outline printed for those who want to read it
- biblical commentaries relating to Acts 2
- 'Early one morning' story text (from *The Big Bible Storybook*)
- other children's Bibles and Bible story books containing a version of Acts 2
- 'Pentecost!' word collection
- copies of Acts 2 (CEV) or Bibles
- copies of the 'Pentecost!' ET questions

Busy Zone
- plasticine, play dough or clay
- plastic building bricks
- junk modelling items
- rough hewn wood and small squares of sandpaper
- red, yellow and orange ribbons and flags for dancing/moving with
- copies of the 'Pentecost!' ET questions

Quiet Zone
- a separate area where people can be alone with their thoughts and God
- 'Pentecost!' image collection (optional)
- copies of Acts 2 (CEV, printed sheet) or Bibles
- copies of the 'Pentecost!' ET questions

Share

As your time for exploring together draws to a close, invite your community to come back together into small groups of three to five. Suggest that they share their responses to the questions posed at the beginning.

Giving thanks

Invite the explorers to share their reflections with the wider community, drawing together their responses and noting any common themes that emerge. Conclude by reading Acts 2 again (from the same Bible version used earlier). Then lead your community in a prayer, thanking God for all that he has revealed through this story. Encourage your community to continue their conversations about this story as they leave, and to take with them any artwork/writings/thoughts from the session.

In all you say or do

Acts 18:1–3; Colossians 3:12–17

Themes: commitment, discipleship, integrity

Paul was a skilled tent maker; through his trade and the relationships he developed while working he was able to share his faith in a way that drew others into a relationship with God. Every day, every circumstance, every conversation was an opportunity for Paul to honour God – it should be the same for us. In his letter to the Colossians, Paul outlines a strategy to help us live for God day by day. These Bible passages demonstrate how being a follower of Jesus is a full-time commitment.

Prepare

Resources required
- 'Paul makes new friends' audio recording (from *The Big Bible Storybook* audio book)
- 'This time tomorrow' activity
- 'Take my life and let it be' hymn words
- discipleship image collection
- discipleship word collection
- Acts 18:1–3; Colossians 3:12–17 (CEV)
- 'In all you say or do' Explore Together questions

All available from www.exploretogether.org/downloads (using the code from the bottom of page 32).

You will also need to gather:
- ribbons and flags of various colours and lengths
- basket weaving kits (or a similar weaving activity)
- a selection of paints and brushes
- audio versions of different translations of Acts 18:1–3 and Colossians 3:12–17
- blocks of rough wood and sandpaper
- embroidery silks, aida fabric, threads and blunt needles
- items from the Explore Together basic kit (see page 5)
- someone to deliver a short sermon on Acts 18:1–3 and Colossians 3:12–17 (optional)

Presenting the Bible

With the community gathered together, begin by sharing the words from Acts 18:1–3 and Colossians 3:12–17. Consider carefully which version of the Bible you choose to read from.

Alternatively or in addition you may choose to use one of the following:
- 'This time tomorrow' activity

Without being tempted to answer them, introduce the following questions to your community for them to consider:

- **How does this passage impact your every day?**
- **What challenges and opportunities do you face each day?**
- **Why does God want us to hear these words?**
- **What is your response to these words?**

Pray

Pray for and with your community, asking God to help you hear from him. This time of prayer can be creative, interactive, responsive, meditative or sung. It could also include communion and intercession. Ensure that there is a place set aside where people can go if they feel that they need someone to pray with them specifically. Have a small team of people available to offer prayer if required. Prayer ministry should be available throughout an Explore Together session.

You might like to read, sing or play the lyrics of 'Take my life and let it be' as part of your prayer time.

Explore

Read out your questions from Step 2 again or display them on a screen. Remind your community to consider these questions as they separate into their explore zones. Some may choose to consider all the questions while others may focus on just one. Some may completely ignore the questions and just open themselves up to God.

Invite your community to separate into small groups, around the zone(s) of their preference. Explain that individuals are welcome to spend as much or as little time in each zone as they wish, engaging at whatever level they feel comfortable. Depending upon where your quiet zone is located, you may wish to provide directions and remind people not to disturb one another when using this space.

Colour Zone
- paint, brushes, paper
- coloured pastels, crayons and white paper
- basket weaving kits (or a similar weaving activity)
- discipleship image collection
- copies of the 'In all you say or do' ET questions

Listening Zone
- 'Paul makes new friends' audio recording (from *The Big Bible Storybook* audio book)
- audio versions of different translations of Acts 18:1–3 and Colossians 3:12–17
- copies of the 'In all you say or do' ET questions
- a talk or sermon based on this passage could be shared

Chat Zone
- a separate area with chairs, cushions or beanbags
- a chat zone host who is willing to read the passage again and then lead a discussion around the questions
- copies of Acts 18:1–3; Colossians 3:12–17 (CEV) or Bibles
- copies of the 'In all you say or do' ET questions

Word Zone
- pens, pencils
- plain paper of different sizes, ruled and squared paper
- biblical commentaries relating to Acts 18:1–3 and Colossians 3:12–17
- copies of *The Big Bible Storybook* open at 'Paul makes new friends', or other children's Bibles and Bible story books containing a version of Acts 18:1–3
- copies of Acts 18:1–3; Colossians 3:12–17 (CEV, printed sheet) or Bibles
- discipleship word collection
- copies of the 'In all you say or do' ET questions

Busy Zone
- plasticine, play dough or clay
- blocks of rough wood and sandpaper
- plastic building bricks
- embroidery silks, aida fabric, threads and blunt needles
- copies of the 'In all you say or do' ET questions

Quiet Zone
- a separate area where people can be alone with their thoughts and God
- discipleship image collection (optional)
- copies of Acts 18:1–3; Colossians 3:12–17 (CEV) or Bibles
- copies of the 'In all you say or do' ET questions

Share

As your time for exploring together draws to a close, invite your community to come back together into small groups of three to five. Suggest that they share their responses to the questions posed at the beginning.

Giving thanks

Invite the explorers to share their reflections with the wider community, drawing together their responses and noting any common themes that emerge. Conclude by sharing Colossians 3:17 as a benediction (using the same Bible version as before).Then lead your community in a prayer, thanking God for all that he has revealed through this story. Encourage your community to continue their conversations about this story as they leave, and to take with them any artwork/writings/thoughts from the session.

Josiah

2 Kings 22:1–13

Themes: the Word of God, forgetting, remembering, transformation

Josiah became king at age 8, and then in the eighteenth year of his reign he heard some words from the Bible. He was so profoundly changed by hearing God's Word, he tore his robes. In remembering God, he led the way for transformation in Judah. Idols were broken and removed from the Temple; Josiah's heart was turned to God.

Prepare

Resources required
- 'Josiah's story' poem
- 'Josiah's story' poem PowerPoint
- 'Josiah's story' poem backing track
- 'Noisy retelling of Josiah's story'
- 'Josiah' rap
- 'Josiah reads God's book' audio recording (from *The Big Bible Storybook* audio book)
- remembering quote collection
- remembering image collection
- 2 Kings 22:1–13 (CEV)
- 'Josiah' Explore Together questions

All available from www.exploretogether.org/downloads (using the code from the bottom of page 32).

You will also need to gather:
- ribbons and flags of various colours and lengths
- musical instruments or alternatives for 'Noisy retelling of Josiah's story'
- parchment paper or tea-stained paper (looking like scrolls) of different sizes
- audio versions of different translations of 2 Kings 22:1–13
- items from the Explore Together basic kit (see page 5)

Presenting the Bible

With the community gathered together, begin by sharing the words from 2 Kings 22:1–13. Consider carefully which version of the Bible you choose to read from.

Alternatively or in addition you may choose to use one of the following:
- 'Josiah's story' poem (you may wish to use the accompanying 'Josiah's story' poem PowerPoint and 'Josiah's story' poem backing track)
- 'Noisy retelling of Josiah's story' with musical instruments
- 'Josiah' rap

- 'Josiah reads God's book' audio recording (from *The Big Bible Storybook* audio book)

Without being tempted to answer them, introduce the following questions to your community for them to consider:

- **What does Josiah's story teach us about God?**
- **How do you make sure you remember God?**
- **How does God want us to help each other to remember him?**
- **How is God's Word changing you?**

Pray

Pray for and with your community, asking God to help you hear from him. This time of prayer can be creative, interactive, responsive, meditative or sung. It could also include communion and intercession. Ensure that there is a place set aside where people can go if they feel that they need someone to pray with them specifically. Have a small team of people available to offer prayer if required. Prayer ministry should be available throughout an Explore Together session.

Explore

Read out your questions from Step 2 again or display them on a screen. Remind your community to consider these questions as they separate into their explore zones. Some may choose to consider all the questions while others may focus on just one. Some may completely ignore the questions and just open themselves up to God.

Invite your community to separate into small groups, around the zone(s) of their preference. Explain that individuals are welcome to spend as much or as little time in each zone as they wish, engaging at whatever level they feel comfortable. Depending upon where your quiet zone is located, you may wish to provide directions and remind people not to disturb one another when using this space.

Colour Zone
- coloured chalk sticks, glue and black paper
- coloured pastels, crayons and white paper
- flags and ribbons of different colours and lengths, for dancing/moving with
- remembering image collection
- copies of the 'Josiah' ET questions

Listening Zone
- 'Josiah reads God's book' audio recording (from *The Big Bible Storybook* audio book)
- audio versions of different translations of 2 Kings 22:1–13
- copies of the 'Josiah' ET questions

Chat Zone
- a separate area with chairs, cushions or beanbags
- a chat zone host who is willing to read the passage again and then lead a discussion around the questions
- copies of 2 Kings 22:1–13 (CEV) or Bibles
- copies of the 'Josiah' ET questions

Word Zone

- pens, pencils
- plain paper of different sizes, ruled and squared paper
- biblical commentaries relating to 2 Kings 22:1–13
- copies of *The Big Bible Storybook* open at 'Josiah reads God's book', or other children's Bibles and Bible story books containing a version of 2 Kings 22:1–13
- copies of 2 Kings 22:1–13 (CEV) or Bibles
- parchment paper or tea-stained paper (looking like scrolls) of different sizes
- 'Josiah's story' poem
- remembering quote collection
- copies of the 'Josiah' ET questions

Busy Zone

- plasticine, play dough or clay
- plastic building bricks
- junk modelling items
- copies of the 'Josiah' ET questions

Quiet Zone
- a separate area where people can be alone with their thoughts and God
- remembering image collection (optional)
- copies of 2 Kings 22:1–13 (CEV) or Bibles
- copies of the 'Josiah' ET questions

Share

As your time for exploring together draws to a close, invite your community to come back together into small groups of three to five. Suggest that they share their responses to the questions posed at the beginning.

Giving thanks

Invite the explorers to share their reflections with the wider community, drawing together their responses and noting any common themes that emerge. Conclude by reading 2 Kings 22:1–13 again (from the same Bible version used earlier). Then lead your community in a prayer, thanking God for all that he has revealed through this story. Encourage your community to continue their conversations about this story as they leave, and to take with them any artwork/writings/thoughts from the session.

God the Creator

Psalm 104

Themes: creation, provision, praise, thanksgiving, life

This psalm is a poetic summary of God's creation. In it the psalmist takes us from the greatness of creation to the greatness of God, every stage of creation giving reason to praise him.

Prepare

Resources required
- Psalm 104:1–30 individual verses
- Psalm 104:31–35 PowerPoint
- Psalm 104 audio recording
- 'God the maker' audio recording (from *The Big Bible Storybook* audio book)
- Psalm 104 image collection
- Psalm 104 word collection
- Psalm 104 (CEV)
- 'God the Creator' Explore Together questions

All available from www.exploretogether.org/downloads (using the code from the bottom of page 32).

You will also need to gather:
- ribbons and flags of various colours and lengths
- a roll of lining paper
- paints and brushes
- washable marker pens or good quality chunky crayons
- sounds of creation soundtrack (eg birds, flowing river etc)
- floral scented candles
- fabric scraps for collage
- items from the Explore Together basic kit (see page 5)
- someone to deliver a short talk on Psalm 104 (optional)

Presenting the Bible

With the community gathered together, begin by sharing the words from Psalm 104. Consider carefully which version of the Bible you choose to read from.

Alternatively or in addition you may choose to do the following:

Before the session begins light the scented candles to create a floral aroma in the room you are meeting in. Lay out a length of lining paper in the centre of your space and make sure that marker pens/crayons are available.
Distribute the Psalm 104:1–30 individual verses printed sheets to members of the community, making sure that each verse is clearly numbered so that the passage is read in the right order. Play the creation soundtrack and invite the selected readers to share their verse.

Without being tempted to answer them, introduce the following questions to your community for them to consider:

- **What is God like in these verses?**
- **What is he doing?**
- **What will he do?**
- **What does God want?**

Pray

Pray for and with your community, asking God to help you hear from him. This time of prayer can be creative, interactive, responsive, meditative or sung. It could also include communion and intercession. Ensure that there is a place set aside where people can go if they feel that they need someone to pray with them specifically. Have a small team of people available to offer prayer if required. Prayer ministry should be available throughout an Explore Together session.

You may like to display the Psalm 104:31–35 PowerPoint and invite the community to read these words together as a prayer.

Explore

Read out your questions from Step 2 again or display them on a screen. Remind your community to consider these questions as they separate into their explore zones. Some may choose to consider all the questions while others may focus on just one. Some may completely ignore the questions and just open themselves up to God.

Invite your community to separate into small groups, around the zone(s) of their preference. Explain that individuals are welcome to spend as much or as little time in each zone as they wish, engaging at whatever level they feel comfortable. Depending upon where your quiet zone is located, you may wish to provide directions and remind people not to disturb one another when using this space.

Colour Zone
- paint, brushes, paper
- coloured pastels, crayons and white paper
- flags and ribbons of different colours and lengths, for dancing/ moving with
- Psalm 104 image collection
- copies of the 'God the Creator' ET questions

Listening Zone
- MP3 players with Psalm 104 audio track download
- 'God the maker' audio recording (from *The Big Bible Storybook* audio book)
- copies of the 'God the Creator' ET questions
- a talk or sermon based on this passage could be shared

Chat Zone
- a separate area with chairs, cushions or beanbags
- a chat zone host who is willing to read the passage again and then lead a discussion around the questions
- copies of Psalm 104 (CEV) or Bibles
- copies of the 'God the Creator' ET questions

Word Zone

- pens, pencils
- plain paper of different sizes, ruled and squared paper
- biblical commentaries relating to Psalm 104
- Psalm 104 word collection
- copies of *The Big Bible Storybook* open at 'God the maker', or other children's Bibles and Bible story books containing a version of Psalm 104
- copies of Psalm 104 (CEV) or Bibles
- copies of the 'God the Creator' ET questions

Busy Zone
- plasticine, play dough or clay
- plastic building bricks
- scissors, glue, fabric scraps for collage
- paper
- copies of the 'God the Creator' ET questions

Quiet Zone
- a separate area where people can be alone with their thoughts and God
- Psalm 104 image collection (optional)
- copies of Psalm 104 (CEV) or Bibles
- copies of the 'God the Creator' ET questions

Share

As your time for exploring together draws to a close, invite your community to come back together into small groups of three to five. Suggest that they share their responses to the questions posed at the beginning.

Giving thanks

Invite the explorers to share their reflections with the wider community, drawing together their responses and noting any common themes that emerge. Conclude by reading Psalm 104:31–35 again (from the same Bible version used earlier). Then lead your community in a prayer, thanking God for all that he has revealed through this story. Encourage your community to continue their conversations about this story as they leave, and to take with them any artwork/writings/ thoughts from the session.

Frequently asked questions

Does Explore Together negate the need for age-specific ministry?

The practice of Explore Together embodies the principle that a multigenerational community can engage with God's Word, learn from each other and grow together.

It is also true that within age-specific ministries there can be diversity of thought, rich experience and God-given creativity for sharing. Explore Together is a rare tool that can be used to nourish all-age community as well as enhance those ministries aimed at specific age-groups.

Although some churches do take and use Explore Together as a discrete part of their monthly programme, many churches use it to enrich their existing activities. The beauty of Explore Together is that it can be used within children's groups, youth groups, house groups, school groups, Bible study groups, outreach groups or even within the family home – in fact, anywhere that the Bible is shared. Its benefits are not restricted to all-age services.

We are a very traditional church community. How could Explore Together work within our traditions?

Explore Together embraces tradition but also pushes the boundaries that can be imposed by those traditions. It can fit neatly into the traditional order of things and can also be the catalyst that takes the community on an additional adventure.

Explore Together can be used to help people understand and interpret the meaning and value of symbol and tradition. A whole range of churches from a number of different traditions have taken and used it in different ways. It offers flexibility for churches and communities to make the time of exploring their own, using it so that it fits their group of people.

Our church has many people/a few people. Will it work here?

Over the last five years we have seen Explore Together used in small groups with only a few individuals and also in larger settings. We have known Explore Together to be used within a family home, and also within a programme at Spring Harvest for 450 children.

Key to the smooth running of Explore Together is preparation and planning. It is important to consider how the participants will arrange themselves into small groups. There is a danger that individuals who are close friends, or of similar age and background, will organise themselves into groups, therefore missing out on the excellent opportunity to learn from those who are a different age or stage in their lives. Inclusivity is key if individuals want to be challenged to learn something new.

While the planning, organisation and setting up of the zones are essential, large or small numbers of people do not present a challenge. No matter how large the group is, Step 5: Sharing is always done in small groups of three to five people. When feeding back in larger churches or groups, having a group of people with roving radio microphones in the congregation works very well.

Isn't Explore Together a bit chaotic, especially with children present?

It is chaotic in the sense that everyone is engaging in different ways, but not because the children are present. The explore zones are designed to embrace a range of learning preferences. Individuals of all ages very quickly find their own preferred activity and become occupied. Although there might be a buzz in the room, activity will be purposeful, colourful and appealing, and everyone has the freedom to move around and make choices in a safe and supportive environment. Many adults find the kinaesthetic dimension of Explore Together appealing too!

Does Explore Together need a lot of space? We have fixed pews in our church building that often restrict what we can do

Explore Together can be planned carefully to fit flexibly into spaces that are different in size and organised in different ways. The explore zones do not all need to happen in one room, they could be spread out to happen in different areas. Your choice of activities can also be tailored to the amount of space you have, and you can creatively use the edges and corners of a room that contains pews. The smallest setting for Explore Together that we have heard about is at a dining room table in a family home.

I find sharing my ideas and thoughts very daunting. Do I really have to share my answers? Will others pressure me into talking?

The value of small groups is significant. Individuals have the opportunity to share what they have discovered, and shape the views, thinking and experiences of each other.

It is important that small groups are 'safe places', and that key expectations for how those groups will function are shared. Small groups need to be a place where individuals might not speak. There is huge value in being part of a small group and simply listening. Small groups also need to be a place where people can freely make mistakes, a place where original thoughts and ideas are encouraged. Some individuals might benefit from talking their ideas through one-to-one with another before sharing in a group, but others may never do so.

Individuals within groups need to be careful not to add to pressure others might feel. It should never be an expectation that everyone will talk.

Is Explore Together an alternative to Messy Church?

Messy Church and Explore Together complement each other in many ways. Explore Together can be used as a way of engaging with the Bible within any context. It is just one way of exploring the Bible 'in community'.

Messy Church is a Fresh Expression of church developed to encourage new congregations previously out of reach of 'traditional' church. Rather than replace Messy Church, Explore Together could be used within a Messy Church congregation. In his book *Making Disciples in Messy Church*, Paul Moore mentions that there is a lack of discipleship resources specifically designed for adults and children to use together in an all-age context, like Messy Church, or in the family home. I would strongly suggest that Explore Together ticks that box.

How inclusive is Explore Together for individuals with disabilities and learning difficulties?

Individuals with disabilities and learning difficulties have been involved in Explore Together since its inception. Those with physical difficulties, Down syndrome, diagnoses of ADHD and autistic spectrum conditions have all participated. Individuals are able to express their personal skills, interests and abilities in the explore zone. They can focus on tasks for a length of time that fits their capabilities, and they can share their answers in verbal and nonverbal ways.

It is important to eliminate barriers to participation when planning. For example, if your church or group has members with physical disabilities it is a good idea to ensure that materials and activities are placed at a suitable height. For others, you might wish to use a visual timetable to help an individual know what will be happening next and to show the choices that are available to them in the explore zones.

Explore Together is a scary concept for our church. Is there any way we can implement it in stages?

The key to using Explore Together is to get to know and trust it. Using Explore Together in a smaller group setting to start with helps to build confidence and gets people involved. Using it in a house group setting or with a Sunday school group provides the ideal environment for becoming familiar with the process – children are so much more receptive to new ideas than adults!

I started using Explore Together with a small group of 5 to 11s. Other members of the children's team were involved and experienced first hand its effectiveness. From there we gained the confidence to share what we did in Sunday school with the wider church community. What started for me within a small group of children has now been used with 450 8 to 11-years-olds at Spring Harvest and in large national intergenerational events, too. If you need to, start small but don't be afraid to grow.

How can Explore Together help adults who are reluctant to get out of the pew to engage?

The first thing to establish in situations like this is: Why the reluctance? If the reason concerns mobility and access then measures can be taken to make sure that all areas are easily available or, in extreme cases, the resources can be brought to the person.

More often than not the reluctance comes from the fear of change. The very nature of Explore Together is to provide an environment where every person can engage with the Bible in a way that embraces their natural preferences. There is quite literally something for everyone – the key is making sure that Explore Together is understood before it is forced upon a community that could be less than receptive.

If there are only one or two people for whom change may be difficult, take some time to sit down and explain what you plan to do and why you are doing it. There should be no pressure for people to go to a zone. One of the options is to reflect on the Bible passage quietly, and people could do this by staying in their seats; another is to deliver a sermon in the listening zone.

If the community is filled with people who are reluctant to leave their pews then maybe Explore Together in zone format is not right for you at this time. An alternative option would be to provide a bag (brown paper takeaway bags are ideal) for each person. The bag would contain a small notebook, a pen, a pack of coloured pencils, a small tub of play dough, some images relating to the Bible passage, a copy of the Bible passage or a Bible and a copy of the questions. The process would be the same, except that the community remains seated while they explore. The sharing time would be with those seated around them, and the feedback would happen in the same way as in the original format. This is less than ideal but it could be a stepping stone.

There will need to be a point at which a decision to move forward needs to be taken. Explore Together is a tool created to encourage people to discover the truths of the Bible for themselves. It is another pathway to a deeper relationship with God, intended to help people grow in their faith and reach maturity. Reluctance to engage should be seen as a pastoral opportunity to come alongside that person; to identify barriers and begin to break them down with prayer and persistence. Discipleship is never a done deal, it is a continuous journey that needs to take place in community. It also requires us to address and not ignore telltale signs that indicate the need for intervention – part of being a biblical community is to take that responsibility seriously (Colossians 1:28; 3:16). Explore Together helps to identify where on that journey we are and where help is needed.

What if someone says something completely off-the-wall?

My immediate response to this question is, 'it's better out than in'. What better place is there to explore your faith and ask your questions than in a community of faith – a community made up of many people with varying levels of understanding, wisdom, knowledge and experience? Explore Together provides a safe environment for people to express their thoughts and ideas, some of which may otherwise never be aired or challenged. The questions help to provide safe boundaries and keep the focus on the desirable aims and outcomes.

The web resources for the sessions in this book are available from:
www.exploretogether.org/downloads

Your access code is: EXP4ORe2gThr